Success Principles from Father to Daughter

Success Principles from Father to Daughter

A Motivational and Inspirational Guide to Realizing Your Dreams

Bernice J. Washington

iUniverse, Inc.
New York Lincoln Shanghai

Success Principles from Father to Daughter

iUniverse books may be ordered through booksellers or by contacting:

iUniverse
2021 Pine Lake Road, Suite 100
Lincoln, NE 68512
www.iuniverse.com
1-800-Authors (1-800-288-4677)

ISBN: 978-0-595-43139-7 (pbk)
ISBN: 978-0-595-87484-2 (ebk)

Printed in the United States of America

For more information, contact:
Bernice J. Washington
Washington Training & Development
18352 Dallas Parkway #136, PMB 340
Dallas, TX 75287
972-407-9090
Web site:
www.bernicewashington.com
e-mail: bernice@bernicewashington.com

To my father, James Jones, and all fathers who have helped shape and mold your daughters' dreams and ambitions. I hope you will continue to encourage them to reach for higher heights.

To Ma'dear, Sarah B. Jones, thank you for being a strong woman who was steadfast, immovable, and beside my father in all of his endeavors. You have set the example of womanhood.

Contents

Acknowledgments

No man or woman is ever an island. I want to thank several people who gave moral encouragement or lent a hand in helping me produce this book:

Lymon, Andrea, and Michael for their undying encouragement and faith in my ability to make a positive contribution by writing this book.

My siblings: my sister, Dorothy Jones Williams, and my brothers, McKinley Young, Isaac G. Jones and Billy G. Jones, for allowing me to be all that I had the capacity to be.

Wilma Teen Flucas for her unwavering support and friendship.

Sharon Egiebor and James Wallace, III esquire for helping me crystallize my ideas and creating an ebb and flow to these stories.

Richard McClure for his patience and dedication in using his graphic skills to present a polished product.

Ruth McClure for her inspirational photos.

Thanks to all.

Introduction

I'm a daddy's girl. Wherever Daddy went, I wasn't far behind. When folks saw James Jones coming, they automatically looked down for me. Now, it didn't matter if he was going to the cotton fields, to the woods to hunt for our family supper or just to the country store. I had to be with him. We shared the same interests, had similar temperaments and yes, we favored each other so much that it even looked like he spat me out.

Daddy loved all of his children equally—McKinley, Isaac, Dorothy, Billy and me—and we loved him. But for me, Daddy was the creator of all that was good. Next to God, I didn't know another man who could be so wise, loving, caring, and generous until I married my husband, Lymon.

Daddy inspired me to reach high, aim for the stars, and settle for nothing less than the warmth and glow of the sun and the moon. He persevered through some of life's harshest storms and still found the golden pot of success at the end of the rainbow.

He taught me by example how to succeed. Most of these lessons were slipped in as we slopped hogs, fed the chickens, or hunted for the family dinner. The two of us spent a lot of time sitting at the dining room table late at night when the house was quiet. Daddy had created this table from leftover plywood and metal. The chairs were covered with brown and white spotted cowhides, because nothing went to waste at our home.

Some people may think of rural life as poor living. Don't get me wrong, it was hard and it certainly wasn't glamorous. The storms of life, from losing a crop in the wind to having the sheriff arrest my brother, all battered our door. But through those hard times I learned how to batten down the hatches, plan ahead, and find the path that would lead me out of the smoldering Louisiana cotton fields. Daddy, who never graduated from high school, was a leader, organizer, and well-loved and respected member of our community. He became the first black deputy sheriff of Bossier Parish at a time when African Americans were struggling for equal rights in America.

His life was an example of how to *Ride Thunder* and come out on the front end of life by *Catching* the next bolt of *Lightning*. My father was a master at riding out life's hard times and grabbing ahold of the lessons that they taught. I followed his path and caught my own rainbow. I am the highest-ranking woman of color at a multi-billion dollar international pharmaceutical company. I am a successful business woman, civic volunteer who have served on many influential Board of Directors, wife and mother. Winds may blow and billows will roll, but if you take the time-tested principles of success that I'm going to share with you—ethics, integrity, self-esteem, attitude and character—you too can weather the downside.

The secrets to success and prosperity are no longer found only in the traditional canons of business etiquette or from financial trends and forecasting. So this book, just like my Daddy, blazes its own trail in the way it presents success principles.

While you learn about Big Red's or Bobo's antics, you will become a stronger leader, expand your horizons as a team member and create breakthroughs to business and personal success. The end of each story lists the lessons I learned, but read closely and you'll see others. The stories are based on my recollections of life in rural Louisiana. Not everything Daddy said was original, but the way he presented it and his personal walk through life show that wisdom lives forever.

As a child I was told to make something of myself, to dream the impossible, to become a success. I had no earthly idea what success was. I didn't know what *something* was. Of course I had dreams as everybody does. But I just didn't know exactly what to do to make them materialize. I didn't see many people around me who had figured it out. So I wondered if there really was an answer.

After years of wondering, both literally and figuratively, I discovered that I was waiting for somebody else to answer a question that only I could answer. Just like the fictional Dorothy, who had to travel to Oz and back, we search the world looking for something that is right inside of us all the time.

The accomplishments of the human mind and the magnitude of our accumulated knowledge are astounding. Mankind has traveled through deepest space, created pyramids, and deciphered the human genome.

Why then, if the human mind is so ingenious, can we not conceive a simple idea? If our minds can conceive it and our hearts can believe it, then it is possible for us to achieve it.

"Our deepest fear is not that we are inadequate. Our deepest fear is that we are powerful beyond measure. It is our light, not our darkness, that most frightens us" (Nelson Mandela).

Out of my cotton field experience, my personal vision was born—get the heck out of this field. This book is my way to share what I have learned. It will open your eyes to new ways of envisioning the challenges of today's world. Success

Principles from Father to Daughter empowers you to transform your organization, your career, and yourself. The success principles can raise your self-esteem, improve personal performance, and give you complete control over every aspect of your personal and professional life.

Your cotton field may be that dead-end job, an unfilled desire to become an entrepreneur, the need to build a cohesive team, or a way to take your company to the highest level of achievement possible.

These success principles will help you to …

- Understand the value of your attitude in achieving goals
- Improve your self-confidence
- Develop your leadership skills
- Challenge your view of change
- Identify your vision and mission
- Assess your commitment and limits to attaining success

Now is the time to envision your dream, set your goals, and obtain the impossible.

Why not start from where you are today?

Time

I am nothing,
yet I'm valued so much.
I cannot be seen, held, heard or touched.
Yet I am the ruler of so many,
And the friend to so few,
And you care for me,
Much more than I care for you.
I am your constraint,
The cause of much strain.
To some I am money,
To others years of pain.
And in your final seconds,
I'll still be on your mind
Who am I?
Think quickly … hurry … too late …
You're out of time.

James Wallace III, esquire

*Printed with permission

Chapter 1
Change: Handling the Inevitable

We lived on a speck of land so deep into northern Louisiana that God had to get up an extra hour early just to pump sunlight and air back to us.

How deep? Well, now ... most folks who know anything about Louisiana know how to get to Shreveport, just a few minutes east of the Texas border. Bossier City is just outside of Shreveport. If you happen to know where Bossier City is, then Princeton is just outside of Bossier City. And of course, Haughton is just outside of Princeton, and Koran is just outside of Haughton. We lived in a little community called Goat Hill that is just outside of Koran. You get the point ... we were real rural.

Nowadays, most folks are beating a path down to the boats in Bossier City. They try their hand at 21, turn that roulette wheel or yank those slot levers. Ka-ching! Ka-ching! We all know that if you haven't been, you've certainly heard about it. Uh huh.... Just keep driving by all those Las Vegas-style, eye-popping, glittery lights, because there's a way to go to get to Goat Hill. You do remember that Bossier City is outside of Princeton, which is outside of Haughton, which is outside of Koran, which is outside of Goat Hill.

The fields spread wide open and the highway noise dissipates. If you happen to be driving at night, the big city lights will disappear as the four-lane highway eases into a small, two-lane road. The peace and serenity of rural life creep over the skin like the sweet caress of a mother's loving arm. That's Haughton, and Koran is close. And as you start thinking you're driving into no-man's land, you'll hit Goat Hill, regally rising above a Red River tributary.

We've lived here for generations. The 3.5 acres on which Daddy James Jones and neighbors built our house from the ground up was purchased from Grandpa Joe Jones. We were surrounded by the love of family—first cousins, second cousins, and cousins once removed, along with the aunts, uncles, and friends who felt like family.

I'm a country girl who learned values and ethics while sitting at Daddy's knee. He was a treasure trove of information. He used the simplicity of rural life—milking the cows, picking cotton, caring for the animals—as a textbook.

What he didn't learn from day-to-day working, he picked up watching the news and taking correspondence courses.

Daddy believed the impossible dream becomes possible, if it is undergirded by preparation, perspiration, and inspiration. His principles sculpted my thoughts, ambitions, visions, and views of the world.

He peppered these principles throughout my life, providing a solid foundation for my future. They have proven to be the bedrock for success and prosperity in my business and personal life.

He was an ordinary man with extraordinary wisdom, who often said, "My teachers are common sense and imagination. These twins have allowed me to transcend the restrictions of time and space and find myself within me."

One of my toughest lessons involved the goats that lived in our community.

Every morning before daybreak a herd of about twenty to thirty goats would graze on the hills overlooking the river. Oh, what a majestic sight! You could see a silhouette of the goats splashed across the canvas of the early morning sky. As the climbing sun painted a gold and gray backdrop, the white-furred goats emerged brilliant in the foreground. I would wake in the morning to the sounds of the goats as they grazed on the hill. Even Rembrandt would have marveled at this magnificent work of nature.

Now these goats had been climbing that steep hill for years. This is how the town got its name. But when I was in my teens, the neighbors at the bottom of the hill said the goats had to go.

"GO? You must be kidding." I had become attached to those goats. Watching them in the morning helped get my day started. A protest movement—a crusade of a grand order—was needed. I began rallying the neighbors.

Oh, how I talked and talked and talked. I tried cajoling and pleading. "Enough!" the neighbors said. A delegation came up the hill and called us out.

Daddy was a leader in our community of ninety or so people. Even though he only had an eleventh grade education, he was known for his no-nonsense approach to problems and willingness to stand up for others. Folks saw him as a hard worker and good family man. That evening, Daddy and I had one of our infamous after-dinner table discussions. Just him and me. No mother. No sister. Not even my baby brother playing nearby.

Being from the country, Daddy didn't always use perfect English, but his messages were always crystal clear.

"Bernice," he said. "You ever thought 'bout where those goats go when they leave Goat Hill?"

"No, Daddy. But Daddy, the goats are beautiful. You see them in the morning, don't you?"

"Those goats go down in the bottoms and eat the crops our neighbors have planted. Those crops are their livelihood. Those goats are valuable to our community but they're causing some problems. We've got to decide how to balance them two things. How do we keep the goats but still 'liminate the problems they cause?"

He went on to explain that the goats weren't wild, free beings as I had thought, and that the musty odor offended most folks who were down wind of them. His ways were patient and caring. Together we decided to seek a compromise.

You see every problem has a solution if we look for it, and most solutions require change. As beautiful as those goats were to me, I needed to see them from the perspective of the community. Those goats, which had been there for years, were not in the right place. For the good of the community, something had to change. We constructed a fence around the area where the goats grazed, limiting their ability to intrude on our neighbors.

We face change everyday—in our personal life and in the work place. Many times we fear those changes because we don't understand what is down the road. Take the time to listen to the other side, appreciate what you have for the moment, but know when to let go.

It's O. K. to be anchored in the past as long as your are focused on the future. It is important to be prepared to adjust your sails to reach your destination because you can not control the direction of the wind. Do an honest assessment of where you are TODAY and plan where you want to be tomorrow. Successful people may be on the right track, but they will get run over if they just stand still.

"The impossible dream becomes possible, if it is under girded by preparation, perspiration, and inspiration."

Chapter 2
Self-confidence: Discovering Who You Are

Life in Goat Hill was hard, but full of simple pleasures. Daddy worked as an overseer at the plantation's alfalfa mill in the bottoms. Ma'dear took care of the house, me, my sister Dorothy, and my brothers Isaac and Billy. McKinley, the eldest son, had moved to California to make his own way in life.

Like the biblical Garden of Eden, the land gave us everything we needed. The rich, red clay spewed forth vine-ripened tomatoes as big as your hand, black-eyed peas (that were perfect with ham hocks), yellow squash, greens ... and all sorts of other vegetables.

We had cows for milk, hogs for meat, and mules to help us plow. The woods were full of nature's bounty. Our house was built with the lumber milled from the surrounding forest. Daddy's work-worn hands crafted our wood and metal dining room table and the shelves that held our clothes.

Mmm, mmm, it was some good living. So, you can imagine my surprise the day I found out we were poor. Yep, poor!

"Bernice you are poor. Your mama and daddy are poor, and your sister and brothers are poor," the kids at school said. "Your entire family is poor."

I burst into tears and cried hysterically at this cruel revelation. Until that moment, I didn't *know* that we were poor!

I was wearing the cutest thing that day. I had nearly jumped for joy when Cousin Ira Mae gave me this gorgeous piece—the material featured a pink background with blue and green flowers in a Hawaiian-style design. It was the nicest thing I had. Dorothy and I made all of our clothes and this was one of the few store bought outfits that I owned. I took special care that morning to fix my hair and clean my shoes. Passing the mirror on the way out of the door, I took another glance. Oh, yeah, I looked good.

Goat Hill had no school of its own. We were bussed about 20 miles into Princeton, our version of uptown, city life. The segregated school had the city folks, the rural or suburban folks, and us, fresh off the farm.

Those city kids took one look at my outfit and they laughed. I'm not talking about heh, heh, heh, smile-behind-your-hand tittering. No, they guffawed and belly-laughed. And they were still chuckling at the end of the day.

I was in junior high school and had never much worried about what other people thought of me. Daddy had taught me to stand tall, to be myself. "Bernice, you are no better than anybody else, but nobody is better than you," he would say.

Here I was, wearing the most beautiful dress in the world and feeling like Miss America, only to find out it was a slip. Yes, a slip made to wear UNDER your clothes!

I was in hysterics. School let out at 3:00 P.M. The bus ride from Goat Hill to Princeton was a 45-minute trip.

Daddy got home about 5:30 P.M., and you know where I was? Sitting on the porch crying. Boo-hooing almost uncontrollably. Those kids had shaken my world.

"What's the matter, Bernice?" Daddy asked in his kind, gentle way.

"Daddy, the kids at school said that we are poor. They said that you and Ma'dear are poor and all of us are poor."

He pulled me into his big, strong arms and hugged me so tight that I could hardly breathe.

Then he pushed me away the full length of his long, sinewy arms, looked me straight in the eyes, and said, "Baby, we're not poor, we just don't have any money."

He went on to say, "We've got each other. We've got our health and strength, and if we work real hard, someday we will have some money.

"It's true that your mother and I don't have a lot of material things to give, but we are giving you the most valuable thing that we possess and that's our name. We're giving it to you clean. We expect you to bring it back clean."

I drank deeply from his font of knowledge, soaking up his wisdom. I never thought of being poor in the same light again. Daddy's words were all the richness I needed.

That day I learned not to allow anyone else to define who I was. Self-validation is more important than external evaluation.

As I reflect on my father's words, I see now that *poor* is a relative term.

Just as *poor* is a relative term, so is *success*. Success means more than material things—*more* does not necessarily equal *better*.

Success is creating a vision and then carefully crafting it to determine the path you must travel to achieve your dreams.

What exactly is a vision? Daddy's vision was to see his children experience a better life than he did.

However, it was *not* his vision to see us live life without hardship or challenges. Anything worth having is worth working for, we were told.

He insisted that all that the world owes you is a chance. What you do with that chance is your choice.

The world owes you a chance to dream and work at making those dreams come true.

A chance to succeed or fail on your own merits.

A chance to stand up when you want to sit down.

He went on to assure us that there is no such thing as a free lunch … every now and then, you may get a dessert for free … but you've got to pay for your lunch.

He insisted that Ma'dear and he were going to give us that chance. But we had to choose how to use it.

"This is your trip around the track. Neither your mother nor I can run it for you. All we can do is see to it that you have the proper equipment. We are prepared to provide you with that equipment. How or whether you choose to use it is absolutely your choice."

"Don't ask anybody to do for you what you can do for yourself. You are responsible for you, and you shouldn't place that burden on anybody else."

Decide who you are, create your vision, and go out and grab life. Knowing who you are will provide the confidence to try your hand at the impossible. The vision will give you direction. Dream the unimaginable and savor life with gusto.

We are giving you the most valuable thing that we possess and that's our name. We're giving it to you clean. We expect you to bring it back clean."

Chapter 3
Goals: Finding Your Vision

Money was the one thing we couldn't grow on the farm. We were cash poor. Daddy figured that working was the only way to fix that problem. Daddy believed in hard work. No, he was an ad-vo-cate for hard work. It was his position that hard work builds character.

Our options were limited in rural Louisiana in the 1950s and 1960s. Unlike today, where teenagers get hired at the mall or a fast-food restaurant, our only option was the cotton field. In other words, we had plenty of character-building opportunities. If there is anything harder than working in the cotton field in 105 degree heat, I don't want to know.

The area along the Red River was one of the state's main cotton-growing sections. Here, cotton was the financial thread that held our community and the state economy together. Ma'dear and Daddy planted half an acre of cotton on our own property, but it didn't generate enough income to buy a flea. While Daddy worked at the mill during the day, Ma'dear, Isaac, Billy,

Dorothy, and I spent our summers working the fields of nearby cotton growers. In the evenings, Daddy would come home and work our half-acre. We were a team and everyone, from the eldest to the youngest, pitched in.

Daddy earned $37.50 per week as overseer at the alfalfa mill. Each of us working 10-hour days earned $17.50 per head, per week. You can do the math and see why we worked. That money got us through the winter, allowed my parents to save for a rainy day, and helped with our school expenses.

Some kids had to work well into the school year. But Daddy said education was more important than the temporary gains of working cotton. Nothing was to get in the way of our ticket to a better future. "Always bury your treasures in your head," he said, "because if you place them there no one can ever rob you of them." Our field labor was strictly limited to school vacations, weekends, and the long, hot-as-a-griddle summer.

Come 5:00 A.M. in mid-July you could find us crawling into the back of an open bed pickup truck with eighteen other field hands. Upon arriving at our designated field, we slithered off the back and stood to be counted. The foreman then handed each person a razor-sharp hoe, the tool for the day.

Cotton is like a jealous lover, over-demanding, constantly calling. It won't be ignored. To get a good crop, you have to plant in the spring, and weed, prune, and water all summer. You pick it by hand in the fall. The white fluffy bolls are picturesque, if you're not in the middle of them with a hoe in one hand and a back so sore from bending you can't stand straight.

Each of us was given a three-mile row to be weeded by 6:00 P.M. quitting time. The first time I looked down the long, long row, I thought, there ain't no way I can get to the end. I had to learn that getting up is the first step to reaching your destination. Miz Becky, who had been working the fields most of her life, set the pace for the crew. She started swinging that hoe, carefully hitting the roots of the Bermuda grass strangling the life from the cotton plants. By 10:00 A.M. the sun smiled broadly over the horizon; the temperature rose upward—15 degrees, 20 degrees higher.

Miz Becky swung that hoe, chopping those weeds. The crew followed her lead. Swing, chop. Swing, chop. Swing, chop. At noon, the sun blazed dead center above us. My arms ached. Miz Becky had moved ahead at least an eighth of a mile. By sundown, Miz Becky would be a quarter mile ahead.

I knew after the first few hours that I didn't want to spend my life in the cotton field. It was *my opinion* that hard work may indeed be a character builder; however, adding the appropriate measure of mental competency could contribute to reducing the necessity for *100 percent physical* labor. In other words, I knew I'd have to find me a way out of this field.

Field work left you sweaty, dusty, and dog-tired. Perspiration clung to your skin. Wearing short sleeves and cut-off shorts had to be cooler. I took this proposition to my mother. She insisted that I continue wearing long-sleeved shirts and pants. We conversed on this point for about 15 minutes as my father listened.

After a more heated exchange, he placed his hand on my mother's shoulder and said, "Sarah, Bernice don't believe fat meat is greasy. Let her have her way." Ma'dear didn't say another word. At last, Daddy understood *my* logic and was siding with me.

The next day, I wore a short-sleeved shirt and old, tattered, cut-off blue jeans to the field. Trendsetter that I was, my fellow workers certainly would copy my ingenious attire.

About noon, as that sun started sending out heat waves, my skin began to burn and turn colors like a chicken roasting in the oven. Blisters formed on my arms and legs. For some reason, I was hotter without the long sleeves and long pants.

I looked across the field. Daddy was driving up in his pickup truck. What a relief! He frequently checked on us in the middle of the day. I broke into a Cheshire cat grin because I knew that he must have anticipated my plight and had come to rescue me.

He looked at me sympathetically and said, "Now you know what you mama was trying to tell you, don't ya?" I hurriedly acknowledged my error and waited for him to take me home to change.

"A hard head makes a soft booty," he said, climbing back into his pickup truck and driving off. I couldn't believe it. My own father was leaving me to fry in the blazing sun.

At that moment I believed my goal of getting out of that cotton field never would be realized.

I was hotter than a catfish frying in hot grease. Where is that water boy? I said to myself. I'm so thirsty I can't think. But the water boy was dancing to different music. His job was to move from one field hand to another, offering the long awaited chilled water.

After each serving, he placed the dipper back into the bucket, retrieved another precisely measured portion and passed the dipper to the next anxiously waiting drinker. He repeated this ritual 50-60 times, until the entire crew had been served. He was miles away from me. My turn was a long way off.

This is a little rhyme used by field hands that describes their job.

My Job

It's not my place to run this train;
The whistle I cannot blow.
It's not my place to say how far
This train's allowed to go.
It's not my place to shoot the steam
Nor even clang the bell.
But just let the darn thing jump the tracks
And see who catches _ _ _ _.

Author unknown

Well … you get the point. Like many, you may have the feeling that you are not running your life. Your life is running you.

After dinner that night, my mother rubbed Vaseline all over my blistered body. When she had finished, my father called me to his side. He explained that life is about choices and choices have consequences. Once you make a decision, you must be prepared to live with the results … good or bad. "You make your bed and you lie in it."

Each of us must decide for ourselves: Is our goal to continue to be as good as we are? Or is our goal to become the best that we have the capacity to be?

Working in the cotton field taught me respect for leadership, how to follow directions, and that I needed a clear vision. Long sleeves, or short, I wasn't going to spend the next fifty years finding out which worked best. My dreams would be built around achieving my goals through higher learning.

"Always bury your treasures in your head, because if you place them there no one can ever rob you of them."

Chapter 4
Mistakes: Repairing the Damage

My brother Isaac was nine years my senior. When he turned 16 years old, it seemed as if he'd lost his mind. The boy started challenging the rules of the house. I think the girls who swooned at his Sam Cook features were part of the problem. Or it could have been that being the star of the high school football team had gone to his head. He was nearly 6 feet tall, had a stocky build, and walked with a swagger.

Most likely, it was just because he was a teenager. You parents raising children know what I mean. Isaac was something else. At 16, he was, shall we say, feeling his oats. That boy thought he could run the house, do whatever he wanted, stay out until the cock crowed daylight.

Well, Daddy wasn't having any of that. In our household, Daddy was the CEO—the Chief Executive Officer—and our job was to *know* that he was CEO. When my father told us to jump, we asked how high on the way up and where to land on the way down.

"I'll send each of you to college once or get you out of jail twice. It's your choice," he said.

Despite his 6-foot-2-inch frame and arms muscular from farm work, Daddy was a gentle, fun loving man. Just don't challenge him. Poor Isaac, he kept finding ways to bring out the General Patton in Daddy.

Daddy ran our family employing the democratic process, but when a decision had to be made, it was understood that he would have the final word.

My mother was the CFO—Chief Financial Officer. She controlled the family budget with the precision of a Wall Street banker. She could account for every penny flowing into and out of the bank account and chifforobe, where she kept our household spending dollars.

Isaac was the COO—Chief Operating Officer. His job was to keep a watchful eye over us when our parents were not at home.

My father demanded accountability for assigned responsibility.

One day Isaac and some of the teenage boys in our neighborhood decided to go joy riding … in somebody else's car. You must understand that few teenagers had cars when we were kids. So the probability of being stopped by law enforcement was high.

Sure enough, we got a call from the sheriff's office.

My father listened intently to the voice on the other end of the phone, his face darkening and his brow furrowing deeply. Five minutes later, he hung up.

He walked over to the hand carved cabinet—the one he had made so many years ago in high school wood shop—and removed the family's savings account book.

Daddy turned to Ma'dear, "I'm going to get my son."

We waited for what felt like hours for their return home.

What was going to happen? Had Isaac ruined the family name? What would Daddy and Ma'dear do?

Daddy wanted us to appreciate hard work because it would serve as an inspiration for us to reach for something better. Stealing a car didn't fall into that hallowed category. Daddy often would allow us to undergo undue hardships so that we would understand just how difficult life could be. I can still hear him offering some of the following wisdom

James and Sarah ALWAYS stood together in difficult times

I want each of you to fall flat on your face while you are young and while you are here with me. I want you to know how it feels to fall and I want to teach you how to get up. Everybody falls sooner or later, but winners get up.

I want you to fall so that I can blunt your fall with a pillow of encouragement, compassion, and love.

I want you to fall so that when you get out into the real world it will not be a new experience for you. You will have honed your skills at getting up and rising like a phoenix from the dust of disappointment and despair. Both will come during your lifetime. It's just a matter of when and where.

It is my hope that you would have learned how to carve a tunnel of hope through the dark mountains.

Never think that you are the only one who faces challenges. Everyone does.

I want you all to feel the pain and the hurt while you're here with your mama and me, so we can put a little turpentine on it and make you feel better. The real world ain't going to give you no turpentine. I want you to scrape your knee but get up. As long as you get up, you're doing what your mama and me expect you to do.

But when you fall, know that we love each of you unconditionally.

Know that all that we require is your best effort.

Know that as long as you are trying to get up, we are with you.

You have to know that our love is everlasting, offered without hesitation or reservations.

Where you are, there we will be also.

Know this without question or doubt.

And we did. Our father's personal commitment of support was the single most important element in the pride that each of us felt as his children.

Finally, we heard a car drive up and two doors slam. The wind was blowing through the cedar tree in the front yard. My sister, baby brother, and I were paralyzed with fear at what fate awaited our older brother once he was inside the house.

Daddy walked through the door first, followed by an apologetic, frightened 16 year old. All the bravado Isaac usually displayed was gone. With his head down, he walked in slow, hesitant steps.

The silence was deafening. You could hear a rat chew on cotton. The suspense was excruciating.

Daddy glanced at Ma'dear.

Finally, the moment came. Daddy turned to Isaac and said, "That's once."

He then turned, walked out of the room, and went directly to bed.

Daddy was a great orator who was renowned in the community for the way he turned a phrase. But that night, all he said was, "That's once."

Isaac knew that Daddy would live up to his promise to send us to college once or get us out of jail twice.

"That's once" meant that if Isaac ever went to jail again, it would be the very last time Daddy would get him out. Isaac and all of us knew *that* with the same certainty that we knew that the sun would rise the next morning.

Daddy made no threats, only promises.

Isaac also knew that he had placed a blemish on the most precious and valuable possession that our father owned. That possession was our family name.

Needless to say, Isaac avoided any further brushes with the law.

Because he knew that:

"It is all right to FORGET your mistakes … If you REMEMBER the lessons they taught."

And I wasn't above learning from Isaac's mistakes. As Daddy liked to quote another great spokesman, "You must learn from the mistakes of others because you can't live long enough to make them all yourself."

My brother's actions had a lasting impact on our family and taught us a great deal about the consequences of dishonesty. If you aren't honest with the rest of the world, how can you hope to be honest with yourself?

Honesty isn't what you say you believe. It's what you model, encourage, reward, and let happen every day.

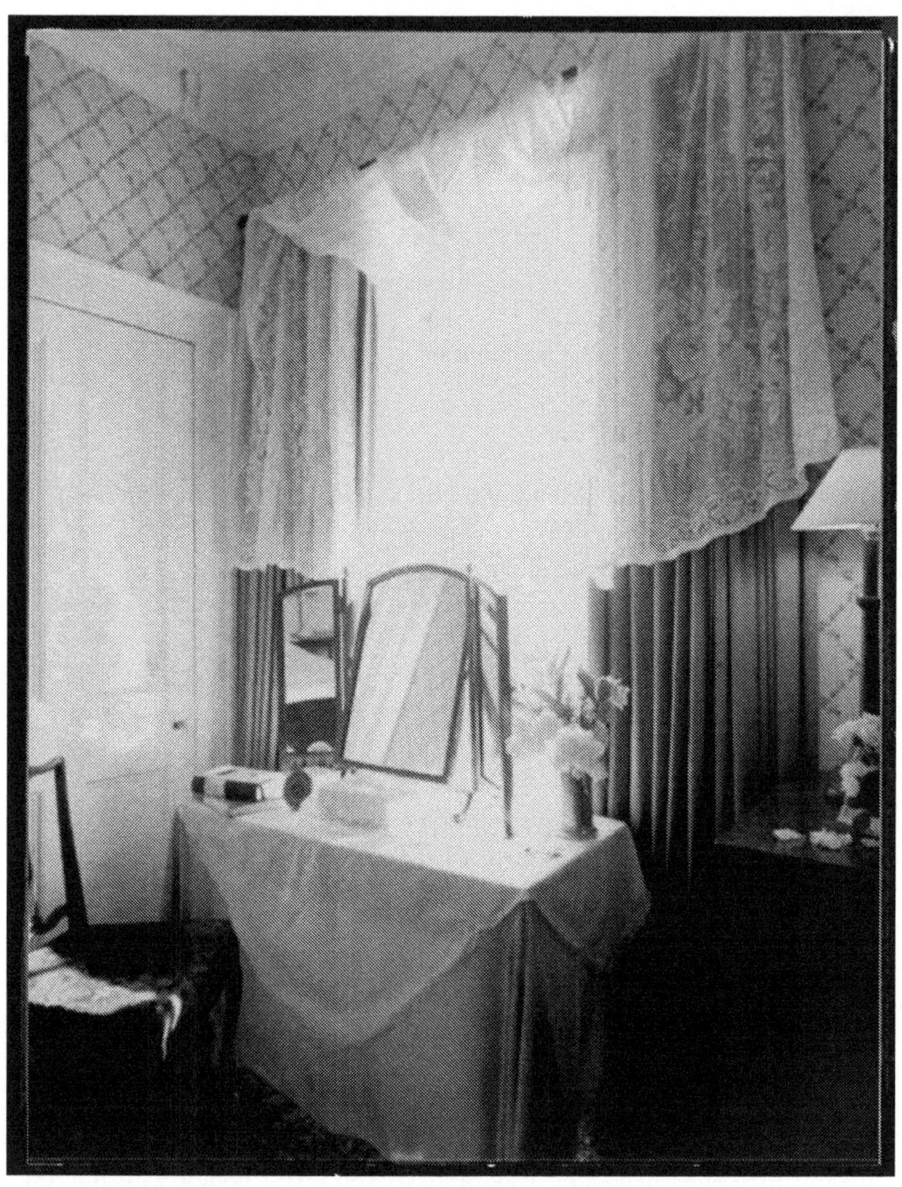

Understand who you are

The Guy in the Glass

When you get what you want in your struggle for pelf,
And the world makes you King for a day,
Then go to the mirror and look at yourself,
And see what that guy has to say.

For it isn't your Father, or Mother, or Wife,
Who judgement upon you must pass.
The feller whose verdict counts most in your life
Is the guy staring back from the glass.

He's the feller to please, never mind all the rest,
For he's with you clear up to the end,
And you've passed your most dangerous, difficult test
If the guy in the glass is your friend.

You may be like Jack Horner and "chisel" a plum,
And think you're a wonderful guy,
But the man in the glass says you're only a bum
If you can't look him straight in the eye.

You can fool the whole world down the pathway of years,
And get pats on the back as you pass,
But your final reward will be heartaches and tears
If you've cheated the guy in the glass.

by Dale Wimbrow

To thy own self be true. If you can't, you'll never be honest in your work, in your personal life or with your goals. Give thanks when you experience the agony of defeat as well as when you celebrate the thrill of victory. Both are equally valuable experiences.

**"It is all right to FORGET your mistakes …
If you REMEMBER the lessons they taught."**

Chapter 5
Teamwork: Reaching Success Together

High school football was the thing that everybody in our community waited for and worked for all week long. Our games were held on fabulous Fridays, a day full of anticipation. All the men talked about the game and all the women prepared for it. When I say big, imagine the hype of the Super Bowl when the Dallas Cowboys, America's favorite team, are playing. Well, we felt that way EVERY fall Friday.

Our entire social life revolved around the game. Since all the teachers were there, parent-teacher conferences took place. That's when the teachers told the mamas and dads what the kiddos had been doing. Depending on the message, that's also when the kiddos found out if they would be in trouble after the game. Friday nights provided an opportunity for all of the moms to do their civic work. They sold hotdogs and drinks to support the team. The night before they had stayed up baking delicious cookies that sold like hotcakes. Mrs. Hudson had the best cookies. She made chocolate chip cookies as big as your hand. Those usually cost a little bit more than rest.

Before the season, Isaac, who was captain of the football team, arranged a sort of football camp. At the end of every summer, just before school resumed, Isaac would assemble all the community boys. These boys, cousins, second cousins, and family friends, all attended school together. This camp was just like the pros do, except our boys went out to a plowed-under, often muddy cow pasture, without the fancy sprinkler systems or the defensive and offensive coaches. Their dedication and commitment were so strong that they also played without uniforms and padding. It was important, no matter the resources, that they be prepared for the season.

Now Isaac's job was to take care of us while Ma'dear and Daddy went to work. When Isaac went across the pasture to practice football with his friends, he had to carry us along with him. He didn't want to be accountable or responsible for anything my brother, sister, and I could have done at home while he was across the pasture playing football.

I went across the pasture to watch them play that game. Being as shy as I am, I just made a *few* helpful observations while standing on the sidelines. What were they doing out there? They were fumbling the ball. They were missing tackles.

"I can't believe y'all out there trying to play ball like that and missing tackles. Oh, you didn't drop that ball … I know you didn't drop it. Let me in the game, I need to play. Let me play. I can show you how to do that. I wanna play! What is wrong with you? Let me play, we ain't gonna win a single game this year. We ain't gonna win a one!"

This went on for about an hour.

Isaac looked at me with this look that said if you don't shut up. I saw him and my retort was quick. "Isaac, the only reason you want me to shut up is 'cause you know I can play that game better than you. Y'all, let me in the game! I wanna play!"

I kept letting them have it. I stamped my feet and waved my arms with each fumble. I shouted at the top of my lungs with each intercepted pass.

The boys couldn't take it anymore. Midway through a play, Big Charlie, our best linebacker, put the ball down.

"Yeah, Isaac. Let her play."

Oooooh, we-e-e-! Now y'all. I'm in the game! I had waited for this moment. But I wasn't gonna play just any position. I *had* to be the running back. The running back got all the glory. The running back could really implement some plays that could break that game wide open. I know a lot of folks praise the quarterback. But it is the running back that makes the real difference. I had to be the running back. I envisioned myself running the ball, the crowd standing on its feet, cheering so loudly it could be heard in the next town. "Go! Go! Go!" I was heading to the end zone and the touchdown was mine!

They let me be the running back. We were ready. We were lined up. The center snapped the ball to the quarterback. The quarterback handed the ball off to me. I took the ball under my arm. I was ready to sprint down the field. I lifted my size 6 foot for the first step, and Big Charlie, who had size 14 feet and what looked like a 50-inch chest, hugged me like I was his long lost mama. Ouch! But before I could open my mouth to scream, all 230 pounds of Big Charlie fell on top of me. I knew how a dime felt under a tire.

As I lay there and communed with the grass, I saw my spirit stagger off the field. I said, "Come back spirit. We've got to stay in the game." Spirit said, "What do you mean we? This was your bright idea to start with."

Finally, after coaxing, my spirit came back and joined me. I lay there motionless. I could sense the whole team huddling around me.

"Is she dead?" Cuz'n Curly asked. "Cuz'n James is gonna kill us all!"

And then, Curly with tears in his eyes looked at Big Charlie, "Big Charlie, you shouldn't have hit her so hard."

"Why not?" he answered. "I would have hit you that hard."

Big Charlie was focused. His whole job was to keep that ball from advancing down the field. He couldn't start majoring in the minors and thinking, well, you know that's Isaac's sister and that's my cousin. He couldn't get caught up in triviality. He was focused. His main thing was to keep the *main thing*, the *main thing*. And the *main thing* was to stop that ball from moving down the field.

Big Charlie had vision, mission, and values. His mission was to make sure his team had an equal opportunity at winning because he was going to do his part. His vision was to see them go to the state championship every year that he was on the team. As for his values, he was going to give 110 percent every time he stepped on the field no matter what it took. He knew his coach could depend on it. He knew that his teammates could depend on it. But more importantly, his competition could depend on it. When a team came to play a team that Big Charlie was on, they had to bring it on, because Big Charlie was going to deliver 110 percent every time.

My running back experience showed me that the game always looks easier from the sidelines than when you are actually in the game.

I started to come around. Tweety Bird was circling my head, but I could hear them talking clearly now and my limbs were moving.

"Give her the ball again," Isaac said.

Now, I wasn't so sure I really wanted the ball again. But I had to stay in the game.

Here we were. We were lined up again. The center snapped the ball to the quarterback. The quarterback handed the ball to me. I tucked it under my arms and made 5 yards this time. All right now. Oh, oh, oh! The sweet taste of success. It was the thrill of victory after the agony of defeat and that was all I needed. So we played again, the next time I got 10 yards and the next time 12.

In life, some days Big Charlie is gonna get you. There will be other days when you make 20 yards or 30 yards and there will be days when you fumble the ball. But as long as you stay in the game, you have a chance to win. Sometimes someone else's faith and confidence in you can keep you in the game, even when you think you want to step out and step off and not be in it anymore. Sometimes people have to be the bridge over your troubled water and just lay themselves down for you.

Isaac was my bridge that day. After the game was over, my big brother Isaac and I were walking home. My legs were limp and my shoulders hurt. As we went down that long dusty road, Isaac put a powerful arm around my shoulder and said, "You did good. You did good."

Sometimes all we need is a word of encouragement from somebody. We need to know that they appreciate either what we're doing or what we're trying to do. And that in itself will help us to achieve our goal.

What you say is not nearly as important as what people hear, Daddy would say. In Isaac's voice I heard all the love, care, and support he had for me. He was proud of me.

Great teams seldom request lighter burdens, they ask for stronger backs. The goal is to design a team that will stand together, or it is destined to fall apart.

"The *main thing*
is to keep the *main thing*
the *main thing.*"

Chapter 6
Finances: Using Resources Wisely

Daddy used lots of examples to help us understand that money was a commodity, one you could trade with and one you made decisions with. His stock phrase:"Be careful not to gamble with anything that you are not willing to lose," could apply to money or possessions.

Whether it was the bike brother Billy wanted, or the pickle in the general store that caused drool to run down my cheek, Daddy made us stop and think before we spent our meager funds. He and Ben Franklin could have had long conversations about saving pennies.

I am still in awe about my parents' disciplined money management skills. Daddy would say, "We've done so much with so little for so long, until we could do just about anything with something."

Those long, slim fingers and wide hands could do just about anything. He could build things, such as the dining room table; repair any machine, including the cars and the tractors; install plumbing, and wire a house. In fact, Daddy and the neighbors built our three-bedroom home.

Birthdays didn't mean new clothes or toys. We received a practical gift like a new pair of shoes or a dress and fresh fruit—bananas, oranges and apples—for Christmas. During the really difficult days, Daddy would say, "Our budget is so tight we couldn't give a crippled cricket a crutch."

When you're a child you only hear, "Save, save, save," or "Don't buy that," or "That isn't worth the money." You think your parents are penny-pinching scrooges who never experienced childhood.

After one particularly hard week chopping cotton, I rushed to the store to buy the juiciest, tastiest, biggest dill pickle I could stab with the long, two-pronged fork. I fished around in that pickle jar until I found the perfect pickle. My mouth was watering and my lips were puckering, just thinking about the joy of that first bite. The trip to the store was our silver lining for working all week.

I headed to the checkout counter that was sitting like a moat around the castle, blocking my enjoyment.

Just as I was about to plunk down my dime, there stood Daddy.

"How much does that pickle cost?"

"Ten cents."

"Let's see. If that pickle costs you a dime, how long did you have to work to earn it?"

I was about 14 years old at the time, and do you think I gave one flying flip about the time it took to earn the money to pay for that perfect, precious pickle? No way!

Even at that tender age I had enough wisdom not to say what I thought.

"I don't know," I replied as my mouth continued to salivate.

"You make $17.50 for working 10 hours a day, 5 days a week. Right?"

"Yes."

"So that's 50 hours a week."

"Yes."

"That's 35 cents an hour, right?"

"Yes."

"So, you had to chop cotton for about 20 minutes to earn that pickle. Right?"

"I suppose," I said, shrugging my shoulders. The math had gotten a little too complex for me.

"Is that pickle worth chopping cotton for a third of an hour?"

"Well … I don't know," I stammered.. "What, what do you think?"

This was entirely too much drama for a pickle. I reluctantly pushed my dime across the counter and purchased my pickle.

But now I understand what my father was really trying to help me accomplish. He wanted to put in place a systematic approach for evaluating the worth of an item in terms of money, effort, and time. These critical thinking skills have proven to be one of the most valuable weapons in my arsenal against poverty.

My father was a staunch proponent of saving. His philosophy was, "Spend some and save some." My parents gave us each a modest allowance because Daddy wanted us to know what it felt like to have something of our own. He told us that he did not want us to be fools over a little money when we got out into the real world.

"In order to manage money, you have to have money," he said. Saving a part of our earnings and allowance was non-negotiable. It was a hard and fast law engraved in stone. It was a mandate that each of us save an absolute minimum of ten percent of any money we received.

He started us off by opening a savings account and depositing the first five dollars. Our responsibility was to grow the account by contributing allowance and money from odd jobs. On deposit days, we would dress up in our Sundaygo-to-meeting clothes and hold on to our piggy banks as though they contained a million dollars. The bank in Shreveport, with marble floors and long wooden counters, was the biggest, finest building that we had ever seen. We proudly stood at the teller window while she counted the pennies, dimes, and nickels, and listed the amount on the ledger.

Daddy would show us the family's savings account book balance on a regular basis. He didn't want us to be in the dark when it came to the family finances. You know, he was way ahead of his time. Most men didn't discuss money with their wives, let alone their children.

He explained that these were rainy day funds and college funds. They would only be used for a life or death situation or to pay for our college education.

Understanding Daddy's reasoning took a while and didn't come without heartache.

One Christmas, Billy wanted to buy a bicycle. He had been scrimping and holding back some of his allowance, but he didn't have enough money. Since we didn't get much in the way of Christmas presents, Billy thought Daddy would be impressed by his thriftiness and would consider paying the difference. It was a stretch, but Billy thought it was worth asking. He asked Daddy if he would supply the cash needed to supplement his funds.

Daddy repeatedly told Billy no. Bicycle money just wasn't in the budget. He suggested that Billy continue saving his money. Perhaps, if he worked at it hard enough, gave up the weekly trips to the store, he would have the funds by next Christmas.

After the sixth request, Billy gave up his plea for additional funding from Daddy for his Christmas bicycle. I had so much compassion for my little brother that I decided to help him. "Most times persistence overcomes resistance," Daddy had said many times. We tried it out.

I went to Daddy and pointed out to him that he had plenty of money in the family's savings account and could withdraw a small portion for Billy's bicycle.

Daddy raised himself from the table, appearing to triple in size and towering over me like a genie emerging from a lamp. I should have thought twice before intervening.

His lips quivered and trembled when he told me that the money in the savings account would be used for three purposes: a real rainy day, sending us to college, and taking care of my mother when he was gone.

"I have to fix this thang for your mama now. When I'm gone, I don't want her to want for nothing."

He advised me against asking for or speaking of the money again. If I did, he would be on me like a tick on a hound dog's back.

It was my firm belief that no day would be rainy enough to cause my father to withdraw one red cent from that account. It would take a hurricane, tornado, and cyclone combined to extract a single penny.

Billy didn't get the bike.

Managing money well was another way of maintaining independence. You shouldn't ask anybody else to buy your dream; you should be able to finance it yourself. Buying things on credit wasn't to be taken lightly. My parents would purchase only one item at a time on credit. They bought a washing machine from Sears and Roebuck on credit, but we didn't get the dryer for a year and a half, till after the washer bill was completely paid.

When I was younger, I thought this frugal living was just plain silly. How do you do laundry with only half the equipment? But as one writer said, my father was ignorant when I was 14, but gained a lot of wisdom by the time I turned 21. As an adult, I found myself doing the same thing. Why buy on credit when you can pay cash? And is what you're buying what you really want to have? What are you putting away for a rainy day?

Daddy would say, "It's a poor rabbit that only has one hole."

By the way, my mother continued to live on the money left to her after my father's death. Daddy frequently said, "We spend money we don't have on things we don't need, to impress people we don't like."

This disciplined response to money taught me to think carefully about my plans. How much is an education worth of my time, my energy? What will I do with the rewards when they come?

"The more you engage in an activity, the better you become at it," Daddy would say. Perfect practice makes perfect performance. Remember, the more you sweat in practice, the less you bleed in battle.

"It's a poor rabbit that only has one hole."

Chapter 7
Leadership: Shoring Up the Team

Every respectable farm in Goat Hill had a barnyard rooster. We called ours Big Red.

He would strut and crow, strut and crow. And when he wasn't crowing and strutting, he was preening and courting the dozens of hens.

Big Red was king. If he were human, he would have been bigger than Elvis. He wore those shining red feathers proudly. The hens would cackle around him, basking in his regal presence.

No alarm clock was necessary while Big Red was around. With the precision of Big Ben, that rooster welcomed the morning sun daily as he bellowed out the announcement of a new day. Cock-a-doodle-do!

A puppy wandered into the yard one day and began to chase the hens. This pup probably meant to have a little harmless play. But Big Red's alarm system went off. Never more than a few feet from the yard, he heard the disturbance and dashed to the scene within seconds.

He lunged his massive body between the puppy and the hens. Frightened, the puppy fled for dear life.

As Big Red assessed the damage done by the intruder, the hens breathed a sign of relief that Big Red had delivered once again. He was faithful as ever.

Big Red had been king of the barn for about five years when a new rooster entered the yard. This new fellow carefully assessed the natural order of things by strolling over to Big Red. He began what appeared to be a ritualistic challenge.

Big Red rose to the occasion. For a few minutes, with their eyes locked on each other, the two roosters went around and around in circles raising and then dropping their claws but never engaging.

The hens looked on with intense interest.

After a few more minutes, the new rooster retreated.

About two weeks later, he returned. This time, the battle lines were drawn. They crowed at each other, bared their claws, and began to dance around, almost like boxers in a heavyweight championship bout.

The new roster charged. Big Red launched his counter-attack. They were engaged in a winner-take-all battle to determine who would rule the yard.

The hens flew about excitedly, understanding fully what the outcome of this encounter would mean to them.

Big Red landed a strike to the throat of the new rooster, momentarily stunning him.

After regaining his composure, the new rooster struck back with a vengeance and drew first blood from Big Red's throat.

Big Red summoned all of his will and energy and delivered a blow to the head of his opponent. The new rooster raced from the barnyard.

Obviously badly wounded, Big Red fell to the ground. The hens stampeded to his side and began to render comfort and first aid.

He lay on the ground like a wounded heroic war veteran. The hens serenaded him for his courageous effort.

The next day, Big Red was gone and was never seen again. The new rooster returned in two days and took his place as king of the roost.

"Daddy, why did Big Red leave?" I asked one night.

"We don't know for sure, but it might have been that Big Red knew his time had passed. He may have been more interested in the protection of the hens than he was in himself being king of the roost. Big Red's thoughts might have been that if another rooster could come so close to defeating him, it was time to leave."

Big Red understood he needed to let a stronger player enter the game for the betterment of the team. This is one of the strongest lessons about character that I've learned. You see, you have to know who you are. If you have the best interests of others at heart, sometimes you have to sacrifice what is important to you.

A leader serves and protects those under his charge, and when necessary, steps aside or accepts a lesser role. You have to be honest enough with yourself to say it is time for me to move on to another stage. You can reach your goals and dreams by giving others the opportunity to reach their goals and dreams and obtain something that is important to them. There is a price to everything you do.

Big Red was my idea of a leader. Leaders have a few things in common.

James Jones demonstrated leadership by what he *Did* rather than by what we *SAID*

Traits of a Leader

They are never so BIG
that they can't bend down to help someone else.
They are never so WISE
that they don't remember who taught them.
They are never so GIFTED
that they won't share their knowledge and skills with others.
They are never so FEARLESS
that they don't play by the rules and live by the law.
And they are never such BIG WINNERS
that they forget what it feels like to lose.

Author unknown

The five most important words a leader can speak are:

5. "I am proud of YOU."
4. "What is YOUR opinion?"
3. "If YOU please."
2. "Thank YOU."
1. "YOU"

Effective leaders are willing to blaze a trail rather than follow paths. An essential element of leadership is knowing where you are going before mapping a road to get there. What you say is not nearly as important as as what people hear. Similarly, what you do must always speak louder than what you say.

"What you DO speaks louder than what you SAY."

Chapter 8
Integrity: Standing for What You Believe

Daddy wasn't always tight with his money. The more generous he became the less we heard about it.

Daddy's lessons were taught in word and deed. But as the saying goes, no good deed goes unpunished. As a leader in the community, my father stepped up on many occasions to work for the good of the people.

He was a steward in the church, a Mason in the local lodge, a community organizer and supporter of almost every good cause. When the church needed funds for a building expansion, Daddy set up his"Bobby-Q-Stand" and sold more ribs than anybody else in Bossier Parish. The catch was his sign, spelled phonetically, that seemed to grab everyone's attention. Who can resist correcting something that stands out so much? Not many folks we know. They came over to correct Daddy and found themselves buying and eating. That was one of my first lessons in marketing. Get the people in and then sell.

Goat Hill didn't have a lot of amenities. We didn't have a gymnasium, a recreation hall, a dance room, or any place that you could just have fun. If you held a party it was in someone's house or out in the yard when the weather was good. The church was okay for small wedding receptions. But you couldn't do the twist or the bugaloo on the church grounds. The only place to have a large gathering was at the high school in Princeton.

Daddy, as Mason Wishful Master, a position similar to group president, took it upon himself to propose that the community build a multipurpose center. It would be on land owned by the Masons and the Eastern Star (the Masonic organization for women), but would be available for community use.

The Saint James Lodge Hall was going to be bigger and better than any other building in our small community. It would stand taller than the alfalfa mill. This would be our Sears Tower, our pyramid, our Taj Mahal and our way to serve the community and bring in fresh money.

The two-story building would hold Head Start and the senior citizen program, and feature an area that could be used for recreation, family reunions, and dances. Oh, the school held dances, but it was so far away that most of us teenagers could never go back to attend.

There was talk that itty, bitsy Goat Hill was reaching too high. Yadda, yadda, yadda. We could never raise that kind of money or pull off a project so large. Yak, yak, yak. The naysayers kept up the murmuring. But Daddy wouldn't hear of it. This center would bring the community together. He helped with the plans and secured the approval of the national Masons. True to my father's financial wisdom, the building would go up as the pledges came in. Nearly half the men in the community were Masons, and they would add sweat equity to the project.

People began to take hold of his vision. By gosh, some said, this could work. We can do this. They wanted to be part of something far-reaching and fantastic. Disc jockeys in Shreveport heard of the plans and knew this would provide them a new venue. For Goat Hill and a good portion of northern Louisiana, this was big. This was the type of project that city councils or major foundations spearheaded. Can you imagine a community of ninety people building something on this humongous scale?

Jealousy reared its ugly green head in the middle of the project. Some people made pledges that they had no intention of honoring. They knew Daddy had put his reputation on the line. He had given his word. Not paying the money or persuading others to back out would make Daddy look bad. They were like crabs in a bucket. Just as one started climbing up that metal pail to join the effort, the others would yank on his leg and bring him back down.

You've met that kind of person at work and in your personal life. You're in a meeting together; everybody agrees on the agenda and the plans. Then they get around the water cooler. And they start gossiping and backbiting and telling how the project is going to fail. "Well, you know Jane doesn't really know what she's talking about. This idea of hers just isn't going to fly. I'm not tying my career into her weak decisions."

The lodge building was halfway up when the money quit coming in. The community was in a quandary. It had taken a year of pledges to get to this point. There was no turning back.

Daddy never spoke of these problems to us. I didn't know the building project nearly failed until I was in the eleventh grade. Sitting around the dinner table, Daddy let it slip how the building got finished.

He signed a promissory note for the loan to finish the building. It took another two years before it was completed.

After spending years drilling into our heads that the family money could not be touched, he used our savings as a guarantee for the community. He also put up our house and land as collateral. He risked everything we had and went against everything he had taught us about money. Our house, the one he had built by hand, and the land that once belonged to Grandpa, could have been gone in the snap of a finger. Years of scrimping and saving and sacrificing could have been rendered useless in an instant.

Daddy had put himself on the line and knew people were counting on him. "What you say never speaks as loud as what you do," he'd say. It was a matter of personal integrity. You have to decide what price you're willing to pay to reach a goal or to achieve a mission. I guess money was the one thing Daddy loved about as much as he loved us. It wasn't the money he loved, but he loved the ability to achieve goals through resources. His dream was on the verge of dying, but it didn't have to. All he needed to do was save the dream by infusing it with what he loved. As valuable as that money was to him, saving the dream and honoring the hopes of the people were more valuable. As he used to say, "Some folk value things and use people, instead of valuing people and using things."

"Some folk value things and use people, instead of valuing people and using things."

Chapter 9
Decisions: Reviewing Choices Carefully

High school graduation was so sweet. I was on my way out of those cotton fields and into I didn't know what. But whatever the future held, it would certainly be better than the past.

There were two things I discovered during my first six weeks at Southern University in Baton Rouge. I wasn't as brilliant as I thought, and Daddy's lessons weren't enough to get me through that first Spanish class.

Even so, I knew I held the keys to knowledge and wisdom right in the palm of my hand. It was within the books.

On my first visit home, Daddy asked what I liked most about college. "They don't have any cotton there," I replied.

He smiled and inquired further, "What will you major in?"

I had only been gone for six weeks. But in those few weeks I had been exposed to Dr. Julia Parnell, my English and speech teacher, and Roena Isabell Wilford, a fellow student. Both were top of the line, sophisticated ladies who had commanding presence. I tried to mimic their diction and mannerisms.

"I think that I will major in theater. Theater will allow me to utilize all of my creative skills while giving me the opportunity to express my inner being. Further, I view myself as the property of the entire world and must give it an opportunity to experience the essence of me."

Daddy and Ma'dear looked at each other, looked again at me, and shook their heads. "What did she say?" They thought I was an alien creature delivered on their doorstep from some unknown planet in outer space.

I could see Daddy was trying to hold his temper, but no matter how hard he pursed his lips, the word came out in a growl. "Theater?"

"Yes."

"Is that something like play acting?"

"Though crudely put, I suppose you could say that."

He came unglued. "Looky here gu'rl,:" he said, with his voice taking a slight rise as he leaned into me. "If you want to play act, you had better get out there in the backyard and act all you want. Just get it out of your system.

"Because if your mama and me are going to pay for you going to college, you ARE going to major in something that you will be able to use to make a living.

"You know that you are head strong and bossy and nobody is going to marry you!

"So you have got to be able to take care of yourself.

"Gu'rl you better get out of my face with that play acting stuff before I knock you back into day before yesterday."

I could sense Daddy was a bit unhappy at my current choice. He thought I should have been more like my older sister, Dorothy.

Dot set the example when she left for school a few years earlier. She majored in English, a nice sensible subject that would give her the skills to teach school. But Dot always was the naturally brilliant, no-nonsense one in the family. That girl was so smart that she automatically rose to the top of her graduating class. "I just happen to know the answers to the questions that the teachers ask," she would say modestly.

Daddy was really proud of her, and made sure that she received all that she was due. When the counselors calculated the grade points to determine who would be valedictorian, Dot had risen above the principal's son. Well, that caused quite a bit of confusion because the principal just knew that his son was the smartest, best looking, most brilliant child ever born and entitled to the valedictorian spot. Un huh.

Daddy didn't wait on Ma'dear, who normally visited the school, checked on our progress, and communicated with the principal, to handle the situation. He took Dot out on the porch for a little father-to-daughter talk.

"Dot, I know this thing is worrying you, but you de best. You're number one, whether they give it to you or take it away from you. When you win, you done won," he said. "Don't fret yourself about littl' stuff, cause littl' stuff, works itself out."

She started to boo-hoo. "Daddy, I just want to be recognized for what I do. I should be the valedictorian and I don't want them to take it away from me."

"Dot, you have fought your battle well. Now it's my turn."

He marched up to the school the next day. That evening, he brought Dot back out to the porch. Billy and I hid behind the screen door so we could listen.

"Dot, I done fixed that thang and I don't want you to fret no more." Dot was the valedictorian.

My father had high expectations of all of us. I knew I needed to reassess my college major. As Daddy liked to say, "Progress is not created by contented people."

I got a copy of the school curriculum catalog, closed my eyes, and flipped through the pages allowing the book to stop where it pleased.

With my eyes still closed, I ran my nervous finger down the page. I was seething. Theater was my passion. During high school I had always earned lead roles in school plays and was a fierce competitor in speech competitions. But I wasn't paying for my education, and I knew that Daddy only wanted what was best for me.

My finger stopped at BACTERIOLOGY/MEDICAL TECHNOLOGY. That ought to please him, I thought.

I went to my father and announced that I would be majoring in BACTERIOLOGY/MEDICAL TECHNOLOGY.

"That sounds good, but I'm not sure that I know exactly what that is."

"Neither do I, but I will in four years." Thus, I came to major in the sciences. It was the best decision I could have made. Daddy knew that it would be difficult to earn a living working in the arts. But a science or math degree would ensure my future. It's best if you don't wait for your ship to come in but swim out to it.

Future visits home from college carried one mandate from my father, and that was that I visit our relatives and elderly neighbors. I would much rather have spent time with my peers who were also home.

The entire community had an investment in my success or failure. Daddy wanted me to understand that if I failed or if I succeeded, I would have to face these people either with my head held high or with it hung low.

If somebody elevates the bar of expectations regarding you, it raises your expectations of yourself. No man is an island. No man stands alone. Each of us is a vital part of the universe of our respective communities. While Daddy and Ma'dear were paying for my education, the community support was essential for my success. My success would reflect on the community. How would it seem if I attended four years of school and still couldn't support myself?

What affects one affects us all. That was the lesson he tried to teach. It may be hard to reach your goals or raise your level of expectations, but if your heart can believe it and your mind can conceive it, you can achieve it.

"Progress is not created by contented people."

Chapter 10
Perseverance: Guerrilla Self-Promotion

Daddy wasn't wrong about much. But when it came to my ability to get a husband, he was way off base. I was indeed a decent prospect for courtship.

Some women sit around, wait for the guy to approach them and then play hard to get. They're so coy, cute, and cowardly. That's not me. I see it. I want it. I go get it.

When I saw this tall, talented titan of a man in a neatly starched khaki ROTC uniform on campus one day, I knew I had to meet him.

It was Monday afternoon and 600 cadets marched down the center of the campus compound. "I don't know but I been told that the streets in heaven are paved with gold," they would sing. "Count off … one, two, three, four. One two three four."

This titan was on the outside, barking orders. Oh, shucks now. Looks like I found myself a real leader. I watched his every move. The men turned at his orders, stopped on a dime when he said so. My heart pounded, my knees knocked, and my, oh my, my temperature was rising. Did the sun get hotter?

I stared hard. Before I knew it, I was speaking my thoughts out loud. "Good Lord! Look at what you done messed around and made! I like that, and if you will help me just a little bit, I can make him mine. *That* young man is a fine specimen of pure chocolate thunder."

The hunt, just like we did in Goat Hill when looking for meat for supper, was on. Persistence, perseverance, and patience were my hallmarks.

You never start a job without doing research. I needed to know who he was and where he came from. Daddy always said, "The hick'ry nut doesn't fall far from the tree." You can generally predict a great deal about a person if you know his family and environmental history. Daddy often said, "You can't plant a peanut and expect a pecan tree to grow." Mother Nature sometimes produces a hybrid that defies this law but generally speaking, it holds true.

I asked around, speaking to other cadets I knew from class. His name was Lymon Washington, Jr., and he was reared in rural Louisiana. He had two sisters and two brothers. Hmm, pretty close to my background of one sister and three brothers. We'll have some common experiences since we're from the same neck of the woods, so to speak. Sounds good so far. He may have some flaws and may not be perfect … but he was perfect for me.

Like any good hunter or general on the battlefield, I needed a strategy. My next step was to locate his post office box. Every student anxiously awaits words and money from home.

The very next day I became a post-it note and stuck myself at his box. I was wearing a yellow dress with matching hair bow that I had made, along with my yellow windowpane stockings and yellow patent leather shoes.

I saw him approach. He walked with such authority—straight backed, arms swinging slightly from side to side. Lymon saluted fellow cadets, greeted friends and fraternity brothers, and acknowledged total strangers with a nod.

My heart went thumpity-thump as he moved closer. I told myself to be patient, to say the right words. I stepped over, making sure I would be directly in his line of vision as he slid his key in the lock. Just before he got the key in, I made my move. "Hi, my name is Bernice Jones. What's your name?"

His eyes roamed from the bright yellow bow in my hair to my shining yellow shoes. "Lymon Washington, Jr."

"Glad to meet you Lymon Washington, Jr. What's your major?"

I know he had to be thinking, who is this crazy girl, because he gave me a quizzical look. "Engineering."

"Good. Because I like trains."

Baffled, he turned and walked away.

The next day, I repeated the routine. This time I decided that I would create a more lasting impression.

When he placed his key in the lock I said, "Hi Lymon. Do you remember me?"

"Beatrice?"

"No. Bernice. It's Bernice silly. Let me help you to remember that. If you put your hand in fire you get a BURN. If one of your sisters has a child and it's a girl, what relationship is the child to you? Niece.

"And if you and I were to get married my last name would be … Wait, let me help you with that concept.

"In order to get clothes clean we put them through a process we call … WASHING. And 2000 pounds is equal to one … TON. Put that all together and we get BURN NIECE WASHING TON. You see?"

"See ya, Beatrice."

We repeated this ritual for several weeks. "You can drive a squirrel to a tree but you can't make him climb it," Daddy liked to say.

Soon all the campus was talking about this girl bent to win the attention of an upper classman. It became the campus soap opera. My name wasn't attached to the gossip. As a freshman, no one knew who I was. But Lymon was well known, especially by all the girls who had tried to catch his eye for the last two years.

I truly believed that if I could just get his attention, I could *get* his attention. So I got focused. "Focus: The main thing is to keep the main thing the main thing." My *main thang* was to make *him* my main thang.

Girlfriends and relatives from my hometown summoned me to their room one evening.

"Listen, we keep hearing about this country girl who is unashamedly hounding an upper classman. We need to know. Bernice, that girl wouldn't be you, would it?"

"Have you seen Lymon? He is so fine. Did you know he was from rural Louisiana, just like us?"

Some of these girls were so horrified that they fled like roaches when the lights are turned on. Those who had the courage to stay tried talking some sense into me. "I don't know you … you're no cousin of mine. I'm going to tell Cousin James."

My favorite twin cousins, Dean and Jean, explained, "Bernice we don't think that this fellow is interested in you."

"Yes he is. He just doesn't know it yet."

I didn't quite understand their concern. I approached this project in the same methodical, systematic, and determined manner that I had tackled any other. It has always been my opinion that a person doesn't have to follow the path but can go blaze a trail where there is no path.

I resumed my station at Lymon's post office box. This time, I was met by his fraternity brother.

"Where's Lymon?"

"He has to study and we're doing him this favor to save him some time."

Okay, more strategy was needed. I reflected on Daddy's words of wisdom. "I cannot change the direction of the wind, but I can adjust my sails to always reach my destination."

The explanation the boy had offered sounded reasonable to me. The next day I waited for Lymon's fraternity brother to get his mail and then followed him. When he handed Lymon the mail, I struck up a conversation.

"Hi there. Do you remember me?"

"Bernice? Isn't it?"

And as they say in the movies, the rest is history.

If you know what you want and why, then go for it with all the gusto that you have. Don't be discouraged by minor setbacks, Daddy always said.

Lymon had seen the light. Amen, brother. Amen. Now it was my time to prove I was right for him. Like my father, he wanted children in the worst way. Not one or two, but boys. I must promise to give him a son.

"I want a son. Now that can be child number 2 or child number 22."

After all the effort that I had put into this project, I wasn't about to blow it now. I swallowed hard and replied, "Your wish is my command."

Education was my priority, so I finished college and then my medical technology internship in Kansas City. We had a southern belle wedding ceremony at St. Paul CME Church, which I attended as I child. Lymon completed his tour of duty in Vietnam and went to work for Westinghouse. Three years passed and no baby. I was getting concerned. My end of the bargain wasn't being upheld.

All good things come to those who wait. Our first child was a beautiful, brown-eyed girl whom we named Andrea Renee.

Three years later, God was merciful and allowed our second child to be a boy. We named this bundle of brown joy Michael Benjamin.

We had someone to impart all the wisdom, knowledge, and wit we had to offer. Best of all, we had love and each other. Andrea has more of her father's analytical mind and chose a career in marketing and management consulting. She is destined to be one of America's great corporate leaders. Michael Benjamin followed my first love and is an actor, singer, and dancer in New York. Equipped with a degree from New York University-Tisch School of the Arts, he is bound for Broadway.

Many people give up because they don't realize how close they are to obtaining their dream. A few more steps, a modification of the plan, or an extra hour en route may be all it takes. Of course the road is rough and bumpy with roadblocks placed along the way. They travel miles, but then they grow weary and quit. Others never start down the path. They don't understand that nothing ventured, nothing gained.

The best way to achieve a goal is to keep going. Know that the cloud hanging over you will move with the first strong wind. But it doesn't have to take you with it. Stand strong, listen to the critics but make your own decision. If you feel you are right, press on to the finish line.

"I cannot change the direction of the wind, but I can adjust my sails to always reach my destination."

Chapter 11
Success: Finding Your Rainbow

The powers that be decided Bossier Parish, which includes Goat Hill, would get its first black deputy sheriff in 1967.

Daddy was the leading candidate. If chosen, he would make history. This self-made man who never finished his high school education, who dedicated himself to his family, and who sacrificed for his community, would be appointed as the first black deputy sheriff in our parish. Daddy's reputation extended into a five-parish area, his community support was legendary, and he had been engaged in several political issues.

Daddy always believed that life was full of unlimited possibilities. "You are only limited by the boundaries you place upon yourself."

But honor or not, Ma'dear wasn't thrilled. "James, you could get shot. You have three children still at home to rear. What will happen to us? Honey, I just don't want you taking that risk. I don't want to lose you."

They discussed the issue many nights when they thought we were asleep and out of earshot. Daddy listed the pros. Ma'dear couldn't get pass the cons. Eventually, they agreed he should take the job. The position was prestigious, he would make more money, and he could help the community. "Progress always involves risk; you can't steal second base and keep your foot on first."

Boom! Overnight, everything was different. We were constantly on guard. Where we had been free to come and go as we pleased, we now called in at night. I was a senior in high school, and we watched our backs at school. We never knew who could be holding a grudge.

Daddy patrolled our neighborhood. We were in the Deep South, with its set of racial prejudices and mores, and he wasn't allowed to arrest white people. The folks he arrested had children who attended school with us. Some of these were relatives. They began putting distance between us and them. All of a sudden we became *them—them children* of the deputy sheriff. Watch out, they may turn you in! Don't say that around *them*. Let's leave. The goody-two-shoe children are listening.

However, we were peacock proud and walked with our chests stuck out. Daddy, after all, was THE FIRST BLACK DEPUTY SHERIFF. We could live with the inconvenience.

Daddy's charismatic personality made him a natural in the job. When a sticky situation arose in the black community, his superiors frequently called on him for the solution.

Bobo, a long-time family friend was shooting up a juke joint one night.

Daddy was already in bed when the call came in. He assured Ma'dear that everything would be okay. He got dressed, waited on his partner, who was another black deputy, and then went to the scene. Now a juke joint was not quite a club. It was more of a hole-in-the wall where folks gather for drinking and dancing. Every now and then they would have live music. This particular one was at the crossroads in Koran, about three miles from our house. It was no more than a shotgun frame building with a rickety screen door.

Two other cars had been called to the scene. They couldn't get the shooter, who was in the parking lot, to put down the gun. The people inside were afraid to come out. Daddy and his partner crouched down beside the other officers whose guns were drawn but not aimed at the juke joint. "James, apparently this young man has had too much to drink. He's firing randomly and nearly hit a fellow a while ago. Folks are trapped inside. Now, I don't think that boy wants to hurt nobody, but he just won't listen to reason."

"What do you think we should do next?"

"What's his name? Yeah, I know that boy. That's Bobo. Listen. Hold on to my gun. Don't shoot."

Daddy slowly stood up. "Bobo. Hey, Bobo! It's me, James Jones."

Bobo replied in a slurring voice, "Oh, hey Mr. James." He stumbled, fell to the ground and another shot rang out as he dropped the pistol.

Daddy ducked. "Bobo, you gonna hurt somebody."

"Naw, I ain't Mr. James," he said and then burst into laughter.

Daddy started to rise again. "I'm coming over there, Bobo."

"Come on over."

Daddy cautiously moved toward him.

"Bobo, do you 'member when we went hunting together?"

"Sho' do Mr. James," Bobo recounted with a big broad grin.

"'Member you tripped over ya shoe string and fell in the briar patch?"

With a childish hearty laugh, Bobo said, "Yea, them briars 'bout eat me up Mr. James, didn't they?"

As Daddy inched closer, he said, "Bobo, your brogans are untied and maybe you should tie them so you won't trip and fall."

Bobo laid his pistol down in the gravel to tie his shoe. My father leaped on top of him and kicked the pistol across the gravel out of Bobo's reach.

"Mr. James, I was just trying to tie my brogans."

Daddy said, "I know you was, Bobo, I know you was. I just didn't want you to fall into that briar patch again."

Daddy sat Bobo up, brushed the dust from his hair, and tied his shoe.

"When we goin' hunting again, Mr. James?" Bobo asked.

Ma'dear nearly fainted when Daddy told her this story. I'm certain that she was thinking that the outcome could have been much different. She continued to support his decision to become the first black deputy sheriff in Bossier Parish despite the personal toll that it took on her mental, emotional, and physical health.

"Success," Daddy said, "is knowing what you want, getting it, and then wanting what you got." He enjoyed being a deputy sheriff. But he also worked just as hard at the alfalfa mill and in the cotton field. Daddy had strong feelings about work ethics.

Work Ethics

If you choose to be a ditch digger, dig ditches with the passion that Beethoven wrote the Fifth Symphony.

Dig ditches with the commitment that Michelangelo painted the Sistine Chapel and carved the statue of David.

Dig ditches with the majesty that Michael Jordan played the game of basketball and with the endurance that Jesse Owens ran track.

Dig those ditches wide and dig them deep.

If you choose to dig, dig those ditches with the conviction that Thomas Jefferson exhibited when he wrote and signed the Declaration of Independence.

Because when you finish, that ditch will be a product of your labor and will bear your mark of excellence.

So let that ditch say out loud and clear, that the quality went in before you allowed your name to go on it.

Let that ditch represent you and the undisputed quality of your workmanship.

James Jones

"If you choose to be a ditch digger.... Let that ditch represent you and the undisputed quality of your workmanship."

Chapter 12
Change: Moving to the Next Level

Daddy was a great hunter. He enjoyed the chase, and took pride in his skills that allowed us to have fresh game for dinner. He was on one of his usual trips in the nearby woods on December 1, 1982.

He started the day at 5:00 A.M. as he always had. He gathered up his weapons, told Ma'dear he was heading out, and spent the day in the woods. Some days he might manage to kill a squirrel or a quail. Whatever he killed, we ate.

It was chilly for Louisiana. When he returned, Daddy went through his routine of putting out hay for the cows and securing the gates.

He walked into the living room and fell at my mother's feet. Ma'dear called the neighbors. They tried to resuscitate him. Nothing worked. Daddy, at 69, was dead.

I tried consoling myself. Everything in me told me that this was a normal process. You expect your parents to die. That's the cycle of life. Yet no amount of education, medical or otherwise, completely prepares you for your parent's death.

For the first time in my life, my anchor was gone. I felt like a ship set out on the sea without a sail. From my view, Daddy hung the moon and lit the sun. I struggled with my own beliefs. Was I indeed anchored by his teachings … or was I anchored by my father? Would I drift off into sea, blown about by each and every storm or strong wind that would come along?

The word went out. Deputy Sheriff James Jones, the first black man hired in the position in Bossier Parish, is dead. James Jones, the Masonic lodge leader, is dead. James Jones, you know, the guy who sells that good barbecue at church fundraisers, is dead. James Jones, Isaac's dad. You know Isaac, he led the football team to the state championship. James Jones, Sarah's husband from around the way. He's the one who's always pitching in when somebody needs help. Yeah, he helped the Mims repair their fence last year.

People gathered at the house. Ma'dear sat in the rocking chair on the front porch, holding court, remaining strong, just as Daddy would have wanted. She greeted all visitors by name, shook their hands, and thanked them for coming. The processional was long. It seemed as if this could go on all night. Our little house that Daddy had helped build by hand was packed with relatives, friends, and neighbors. They had brought fresh vegetables from the garden, cakes that melted in your mouth, and casseroles to get us through the week.

Ma'dear struggled to maintain her composure as she repeatedly said, "It's hard but it's fair." Her once erect shoulders began slumping. Dorothy's husband, Roy, clutched her hand and helped her retreat into the house. All the anxiety and pain of losing a mate of nearly half a century rested squarely on her shoulders. I was of little help because I wasn't much better off than she.

After a while, neighbors and friends began to tell James Jones stories. Laughter rang across the pasture. Remember how he kept that crazy Bobo from getting shot? Yeah, that poor boy nearly bought himself a one-way ticket to the grave. But James, with no gun in his hand, saved that poor chil'.

Remember when Cuz'n James hid under his car trying to scare Isaac and his girlfriend and fell asleep? Next thing you know, Isaac got in the car and almost ran over him.

Hundreds gathered at the church for Daddy's funeral. The building was so packed that at least several hundred had to wait outside. The Bossier Parish sheriff and six sheriff cars led the processional to the cemetery.

After the funeral, we each attempted to resume routines but this proved to be a real challenge. But in time, we found peace and each of us knew that we had been the recipients of the unconditional love of our father.

The Dash

**I read of a man who stood to speak
At the funeral of a friend.
He referred to the dates on her tombstone
From the beginning to the end.**

**He noted that first came the date of her birth
And spoke of the following date with tears,
But he said what mattered most of all
Was the dash between those years.**

**For that dash represents all the time
That she spent alive on earth …
And now only those who loved her
Know what that little line is worth.**

**For it matters not how much we own:
The cars … the house … the cash.
What matters is how we live and love
And how we spent our dash.**

**So think about this long and hard …
Are there things you'd like to change?
For you never know how much time is left.
You could be at dash midrange.**

**If we could just slow down enough
To consider what's true and real,
And always try to understand
The way other people feel.**

**And be less quick to anger,
And show appreciation more
And love the people in our lives
Like we've never loved before.**

If we treat each other with respect,
And more often wear a smile …
Remembering that this special dash
Might only last a little while.

So, when your eulogy is being read
With your life's actions to rehash …
Would you be proud of the things they said
About how you spent your dash?

By Linda Ellis

Though he is dead, yet he lives through me, my children, and their children.

Each day I try to do something that would make Daddy proud. But more importantly, I always bring his name back clean.

Life is all about attitude and how you choose to see things. I could have chosen to collapse after Daddy's death, and sink into a hole so deep a backhoe wouldn't be able to pull me out. Death is always hard to accept. But Daddy taught us to reach for the stars, stand strong when the hurricanes and tornadoes come, and to look for the best in life. I no longer run from life's storms. I'm waiting on the thunder *and* lightning.

My View

I live on the *sunrise* (East) side of the mountain.
I see the day coming … not going.
I see the day as it begins … not ends.
I see things as they might be … not as they were.
I live on the sunrise side of the mountain.

I see hope and have an unshakable confidence in the brightness of the future.

I see yesterday but dream with excitement about tomorrow and what treasure it holds.

I wake up each day on the sunrise side of the mountain, and I choose to live there everyday.

Bernice J. Washington

I believe that:
In EVERYTHING, the *good* is there,
Our GOAL is to FIND it.
In every SITUATION, the *positive* is there,
Our OPPORTUNITY is to SEE it.
In every PROBLEM, the *answer* is there,
Our RESPONSIBILITY is to PROVIDE it.
In every ADVERSITY, the *lesson* is there,
Our ADVENTURE is to DISCOVER it.

Author unknown

Deputy Sheriff James Jones

Seeds of a promise are planted

James & Sarah B. Jones Family Chart

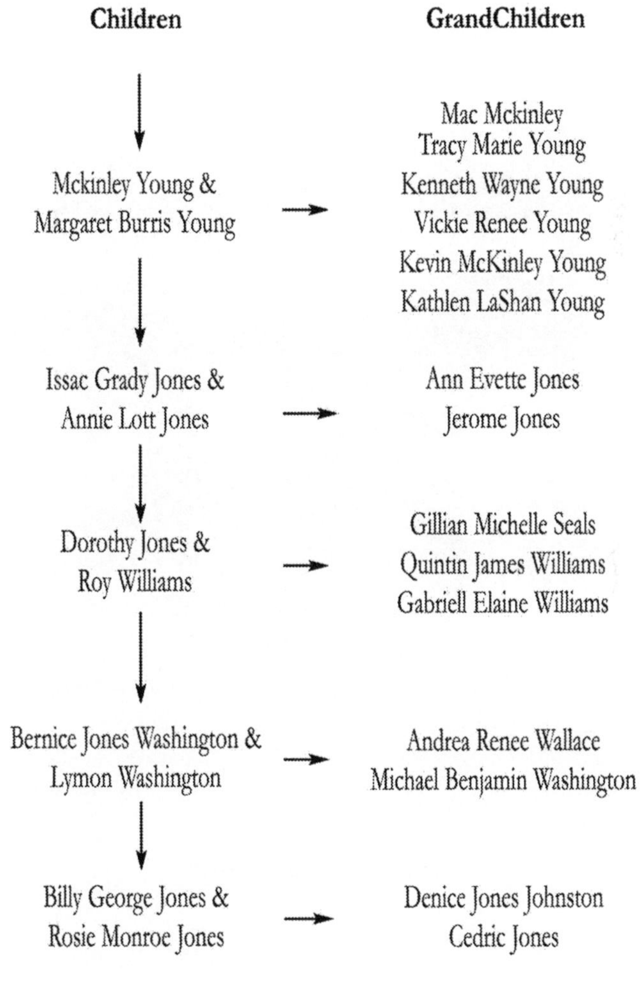

Sarah Blacksher Jones

About the Author

✦

Bernice J. Washington, MBA, CMC
Motivational Speaker/Author/Coach/
Businesswoman

Bernice J. Washington lifted herself from the cotton fields of rural Louisiana to become a successful businesswoman, entrepreneur, and civic leader. She is President & Owner of Washington Training & Development since 1997. She is a Certified Master Coach; Motivational Speaker and Author. Washington Training & Development designs and delivers development and training programs on Staff Development, Leadership and Coaching. Bernice is recognized nationally as a master corporate trainer and coach.

Her corporate experience spans more than three decades. She is a nationally recognized successful businesswoman with a solid background in sales/marketing and management. Her responsibilities include generating more than $25 million in annual sales. Because performance matters, she is a repeat Master's Circle and President's Club winner. She has become the highest-ranking woman of color at a multi-million dollar international Healthcare company.

Also a Motivational Speaker/Author Bernice J. Washington has dazzled audiences across the nation with her unique style and persona. Her dynamic delivery has earned her the coveted title "Motivational Speaker Extraordinaire". She is a sought after television and radio talk show commentator and has been featured in movies, magazine articles and in News stories. She is featured in Southern Living Magazine.

978-0-595-43139-7
0-595-43139-9

www.ingramcontent.com/pod-product-compliance
Ingram Content Group UK Ltd.
Pitfield, Milton Keynes, MK11 3LW, UK
UKHW040558210726
13854UKWH00008B/1487

9 780595 431397